CUTE EMERGENCY

CUTE EMERGENCY

TONY HEALLY

BANTAM PRESS

LONDON · TORONTO · SYDNEY · AUCKLAND · JOHANNESBURG

TRANSWORLD PUBLISHERS
61–63 Uxbridge Road, London W5 5SA
A Random House Group Company
www.transworldbooks.co.uk

First published in Great Britain
in 2014 by Bantam Press
an imprint of Transworld Publishers

A CIP catalogue record for this book
is available from the British Library.

ISBN 9780593074169

Addresses for Random House Group Ltd companies outside the UK
can be found at: www.randomhouse.co.uk
The Random House Group Ltd Reg. No. 954009

Typeset in Helvetica
Printed and bound in China
2 4 6 8 10 9 7 5 3 1

Introduction . . .

Started in October 2013, the aim of the **@CuteEmergency** Twitter feed was to scour the internet to find the cutest animal pictures and share them around the globe. In a world where so much is going on, sometimes all it takes is a cute picture of a dog to make someone smile, and that was my goal with **@CuteEmergency**. Since it began, Cute Emergency has accumulated over 1.1 million followers and continues to grow each day.

The project has even grown to include other accounts, **@EmrgencyKittens**, **@OhMyCorgi**, and **@HereBeHuskies**. With so much positive feedback, we wanted to create a way for our fans to submit their cute pet pictures to us. After thousands of submissions, we chose the best of the best and created this book to share them on a totally different platform. Now that Cute Emergency is a well-known Twitter brand, look out for more Cute Emergency things to come, both online and offline!

⚕ CUTE EMERGENCY

---

1. The cute things in life

2. Something to make you smile

3. Friendship

4. Sleeping in

1
The cute things in life

If I stay still, maybe they won't notice I'm not a flower.

10

Corgi smiles are
the best smiles.

11

A chick's first kiss.

Off to sleep with a hug and a kiss.

12

Sneaking a kiss to show some love.

13

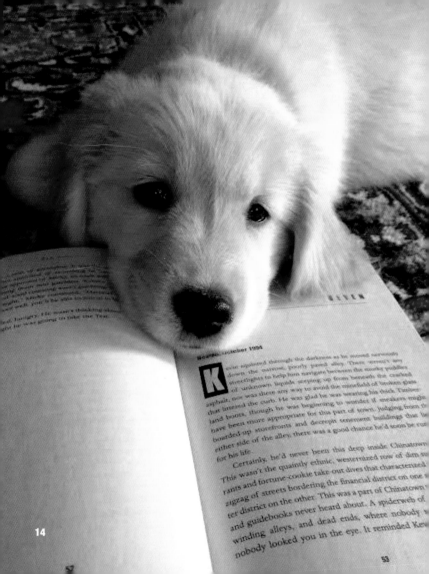

The look of love.

After a long day of playing, it's nice to cosy up next to a warm fire.

15

He's a little shy, so he
hangs out near Mum.

Lazy days are best
spent in trees.

17

Figuring out that paws are not, in fact, food.

19

The cutest shoe
thief ever!

The little adventurer
exploring the garden.

Because everybody
could do with a
personal pocket bunny!

He's so small he thinks his water bowl is a pool!

OK, OK, I sat. Now, can I get up? My bum is cold!

His eyes feel like they're staring into my soul.

Work hard,
play hard,
nap hard.

29

A curious
little white tiger.

He's still a little nervous around cameras.

Balancing work and play is the key to a happy life.

The cutest way to ask
someone to prom.
(Check out his tag!)

Yes? Is there
something I can
help you with?

She's got a bell so she can be heard making mischief in any room.

He's just a
handful of cute.

There's almost too much bunny for one picture!

41

What's up, Doc?

43

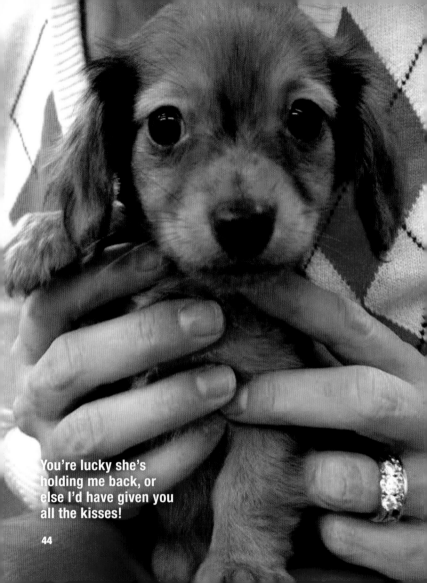

You're lucky she's holding me back, or else I'd have given you all the kisses!

44

Look, I picked my own
Christmas tree!

46

Why'd you have
to wake me?

So, where're
we headed?

With this face,
he gets anything
he wants.

Are we there yet?

Don't forget to buckle
me in ... Safety first!

2
Something to make you smile

I'm getting ready for karaoke!

I will get you for this, human.

Just keep swimming,
just keep swimming!

57

Wow, that's a big yawn!

Me when
I'm watching
a scary movie.

Caught mid-shake.

How you wash a
hedgehog – safely.

It's cold outside, but he's got his favourite jacket on!

He likes to hide in the bath, but has no idea what a bath does.

There're some
new sheriffs
in town.

He's determined
to finish the whole
apple by himself.

Cats love a good
head rub.

I gots a little snow
on mah nose.

72

After years of being cold in the snow, he finally realized why humans wear clothes.

73

He was allowed to pick out his own costume …

If you look
closely, this
isn't a bear.

75

Enjoying the brisk morning walk.

3
Friendship

This St Bernard has taken to raising the kittens he found.

Hurry up, hurry up!

Different reactions to seeing a dog.

81

He thinks the cat
is a pillow.

**Best friends
till the end.**

83

**Best friends
stick together.**

Love is blind.

These cats like to look down and judge everyone who walks by.

87

These puppies like to use each other as pillows.

Playing under the covers is their favourite game.

He wears his
heart on his nose,
not his sleeve!

Who says cats and dogs
can't be best friends?

The three
musketeers, ready
to explore the world.

You can never
get them to
stay still at the
same time.

Enjoying their first date in the snow.

Loving
the great
outdoors.

3
Sleeping in

So tired he couldn't even make it all the way to his bed.

His ears may be perked up and ready to wake, but he's fast asleep.

A stuffed animal helps keep the monsters away.

This is how
he tells you
he's ready
for bed.

With no pillows around, this pup opted for sleeping on his human.

Look at his cute
little pink feet!

He's always down for a high-five, even when he's sleeping.

Synchronized sleeping sisters.

I think a moustache
looks great on him!

Don't step on the sleeping hedgehog!

Gorillas like to cuddle too!

114

116

Acknowledgements

I want to thank everybody who contributed to this book. Without you it wouldn't have been possible. I'd also like to thank those who helped and supported me in the creation of the book, including Elaine, Michelle and Polly. Also my puppy Tug, who motivates me every day to get my work done so that we can go on walks together.

PICTURE ACKNOWLEDGEMENTS

The author is grateful to the following for the use of their photos:

11: *top*, Autumn Dorrough; *bottom*, Alex Wencel
14: Haley Johnson
15: *top*, Talia Godfreddo; *bottom*, Keegan McCanus
18: *top left*, Amy Robinson; *top right*, Emily McDonough; *bottom left*, Taylor Claypool; *bottom right*, Sarah Keane
20: *top*, Christine Tracy; *bottom*, Renaude Poirier
21: Stephanie Gonzales
22: Emily Carias
24: John Keller
25: *top left*, April Annab; *top right*, Samantha Nelson; *bottom left*, khare93; *bottom right*, Amanda Raine
26: *top*, Renaude Poirier; *bottom*, Jennie Baker
27: Shannon Campbell
28: *top left*, Rebecca Green; *top right*, Megan Wade; *bottom left*, Camilla DeCaria; *bottom right*, Nina Verstandig
29: Phil Poe
30: Ashley Marcellus
31: Charlotte Sarkos
33: *top left*, Rachel Stadfield; *top right*, Travis Pettit; *bottom left*, Nicole Berscheid; *bottom right*, unnamed
34: Adrienne Ciccone
35: Warren Davis
36: *top*, Annie Gelhaus; *bottom*, Breanna Galley
37: Ingrid Jungferman

38: Kate Cahill
39: Shea O'Toole
40: Hunter Martin
41: *top*, Zahra H; *bottom*, Eline De Raedt
42: *top*, Jordan Levesque; *bottom*, Tiffanie Tudor
43: Alicia Boulos
44: Hannah Coleman
45: Camilla DeCaria
47: *top*, JJ Lam; *bottom*, Laura Kirkpatrick
48-49: Nicole Chakirelis
51: Sarah Stephens
54: Stephanie Alcaino;
55: *top* and *bottom*, Erik Oehler
58: Emily McDonough
59: *top*, Emalee Bush; *bottom*, Dino Sisic
61: *top*, Kendall Fisha; *bottom*, Nathan Wolf
62: *top*, Ellie Thorn; *bottom*, Lisa French
65: *top left*, Nicki Ely; *top right*, Brooke Murray; *bottom left*, Megan Albrecht; *bottom right*, Kim Trevino
66: Sam Swain
67: unnamed
68: Mark Petereit
69: *top*, Melissa Wiebke
70: Haley Brust
72: *top*, Ellie Stevens; *bottom*, dsp99
74: Zack Pittmon
76: Larissa Lucena
83: *top*, Breanna Galley

Tony Heally is the creator of **@CuteEmergency**, as well as other popular animal-related Twitter accounts such as **@EmrgencyKittens** and **@OhMyCorgi**. Wanting to start a Twitter account to cheer people up, he found that tweeting about animals was the perfect idea. Since then, **@CuteEmergency** has made over 1.5 million people smile, and was even nominated as a finalist for the 'Best Non-Human' award at the 2014 Shorty Awards.